The BIOGRAPHY of Wool

Carrie Gleason

Crabtree Publishing Company
www.crabtreebooks.com

Crabtree Publishing Company

www.crabtreebooks.com

For Judy, Without you there would be no Craig and Aivry - A.N

Coordinating editor: Ellen Rodger
Series editor: Carrie Gleason
Editors: Adrianna Morganelli, L. Michelle Nielsen
Design and production coordinator: Rosie Gowsell
Production assistance: Samara Parent
Art direction: Rob MacGregor
Photo research: Allison Napier
Prepress technician: Nancy Johnson

Photo Credits: John T. Fowler/Alamy: p. 14 (top); david hancock/Alamy: p. 9 (bottom); David Hosking/Alamy: p. 13 (bottom); Chris Laurens/Alamy: p. 13 (top); persis Alan King/Alamy: p. 5 (top); Stephen Roberts Photography/Alamy: p. 1; Scenics & Science/Alamy: p. 12 (top); Stephen Saks Photography/Alamy: p. 7 (left); John Van Decker/Alamy: p. 10 (top); AP Photo/Charlie Neibergall: p. 31 (top); AP Photo/Otago Daily Times,Stephen Jaquiery: p. 4 (bottom); AP Photo/Sedalia Democrat, Sydney Brink: p. 4 (top); AP Photo/Ed Wray: p. 31 (right); British Library, London, UK, © British Library Board. All Rights Reserved/The Bridgeman Art Library: p. 21 (top); Genevieve Naylor/Corbis: p. 16 (top): Gianni Dagli Orti/Corbis: p. 18 (top); Edward Rozzo/Corbis: p. 17 (top); Jean-Bernard Vernier/Corbis Sygma: p. 16 (bottom); The Granger Collection, New York: p. 7 (right), p. 20, p. 21, p. 22, p. 23, p. 24, p. 26, p. 28 (top); The British Museum/Topham-HIP/The Image Works: p. 19 (bottom); Dorothy Littell Greco/The Image Works: cover; Mary Evans Picture Library/The Image Works: p. 25 (top); SSPL/The Image Works: p. 18 (bottom), p. 25 (bottom); North Wind/North Wind Picture Archives: p. 27 (top); Crown Copyright/Health & Safety Laboratory/Photo Researchers, Inc.: p. 12 (bottom); Stephanie Dinkins/Photo Researchers, Inc.: p. 15; Eye of Science/Photo Researchers, Inc.: p. 6 (top); Perennou Nuridsany/Photo Researchers, Inc.: p. 31 (left); Daniel Sambraus/Photo Researchers, Inc.: p. 6 (bottom); Ron Sanford/Photo Researchers, Inc.: p. 30. Other images from stock photo cd.

Cartography: Jim Chernishenko: p. 8

Cover: A Romanian shepherd wears a traditional cloak made from sheepskins worn with the fleece side out.

Title page: Sheep are sheared of their wool at least once a year.

Contents page: Wool harvested from sheep is used to make yarn, which can be spun into fabrics to make products such as clothing and blankets.

Library and Archives Canada Cataloguing in Publication

Gleason, Carrie, 1973-
   The Biography of Wool / Carrie Gleason.

(How did that get here?)
Includes index.
ISBN 978-0-7787-2496-4 (bound)
ISBN 978-0-7787-2532-9 (pbk.)

   1. Wool--Juvenile literature. I. Title. II. Series.

TS1547.G54 2007   j677'.31   C2007-901286-8

Library of Congress Cataloging-in-Publication Data

Gleason, Carrie, 1973-
   The Biography of Wool / written by Carrie Gleason.
     p. cm. -- (How did that get here?)
   Includes index.
   ISBN-13: 978-0-7787-2496-4 (rlb)
   ISBN-10: 0-7787-2496-4 (rlb)
   ISBN-13: 978-0-7787-2532-9 (pb)
   ISBN-10: 0-7787-2532-4 (pb)
   1. Wool--Juvenile literature. 2. Wool industry--Juvenile literature. I. Title. II. Series.

TS1547.G54 2007
677'.31--dc22   2007006982

Crabtree Publishing Company

Published in Canada
Crabtree Publishing
616 Welland Ave.
St. Catharines, ON
L2M 5V6

Published in the United States
Crabtree Publishing
PMB16A
350 Fifth Ave., Suite 3308
New York, NY 10118

Published in the United Kingdom
Crabtree Publishing
White Cross Mills
High Town, Lancaster
LA1 4XS

Published in Australia
Crabtree Publishing
386 Mt. Alexander Rd.
Ascot Vale (Melbourne)
VIC 3032

Contents

Warm and Woolly

From sheep's origins in the mountains of Southwest Asia, wool has become the most commonly used animal **fiber** around the world. Sheep were one of the first animals to be domesticated, or raised as livestock, by people thousands of years ago. Sheep filled important needs for early people. Sheep's milk and meat were used as food, and their skins and wool were used to make shelter and clothing. Today, sheep are raised in almost every country in the world and their wool is used to fill a variety of needs.

Wool as a Commodity

Wool is a commodity, which is a good that is bought and sold. Wool is sold at exchanges, or auctions. Farmers sell their wool to companies that **process** it, and make it into cloth. Wool changes hands many times before it reaches consumers as clothing, fabric, or yarn for knitting.

(top right) A young girl gives her ewe a hug during a competition at a fair in Missouri. The competition involved leading sheep in front of judges while wearing clothing made of wool.

▸ This Merino sheep was discovered in New Zealand. The sheep has been weighed down by its wool, because it had been hiding in rock caves and escaped its annual shearing.

The Culture of Wool

Wool is important to many cultures around the world. New Zealand and Australia are well known for their sheep shearing competitions and their advances in modern sheep farming. The United Kingdom is known for its smaller rural sheep farms and knitted sweaters. In the **Middle Ages**, wool was the most important **export** for England. Wool was so important to the country's economy that a seat in the British **Parliament** was named "the Woolsack." In Central Asia, woven wool carpets are made for homes and prayer rugs, on which people pray. The methods of weaving the designs, called motifs, on these carpets have been passed down through generations of women weavers. Today, the carpets are exported and sold around the world.

▲ *Wool is dyed brilliant colors before being woven into products, like this rug.*

Other Types of Wool

Wool is the covering, or coat, of some types of animals. Sheep's wool is the most popular type of wool, and is the focus of this book. Wool can also be gathered from other types of animals, such as yaks, alpacas, llamas, and rabbits.

◀ *The undercoats of llamas are made up of fine hairs, which are used to make clothing. A llama's outer coat is more coarse and is used to make rugs and wall hangings.*

What is Wool?

Wool grows on sheep to keep them warm. The wool "coat" that a sheep wears is called its fleece. Fleece keeps sheep warm in cold weather by acting as an **insulator**, which means it traps warm air next to their bodies. Each individual wool strand is called a fiber. A fiber is long, thin and thread-like. Wool fibers grow from follicles, or tube-shaped hair **cells** in the top layer of the sheep's skin, called the epidermis. What we actually use as wool is the dead part of the fiber, called the shaft. The living, growing part of the wool fiber is the root, buried in the skin. As the root grows, it pushes the fiber out above the skin. When sheep are shorn for their fleece, only the shaft is removed. The roots stay under the skin so that a sheep is able to grow a new fleece.

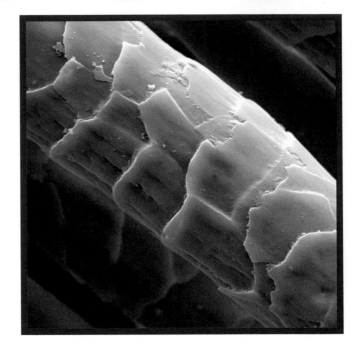

Wool fibers are made up of proteins. This picture is of a wool fiber magnified many times to show the scaly structure.

A Closer Look

Wool fiber is made up of three parts, or layers. The outer layer is called the cuticle, and is made up of cells arranged like overlapping scales. The scales stick together, which makes wool fibers easy to spin into yarn. The middle layer, called the cortex is made up of long, oval-shaped cells. The arrangement of the cells in the cortex causes wool to crimp, or be wavy. It also gives wool its strength and **elasticity**. The inside layer, called the medulla, is made up of spongy cells with air pockets. Wool fibers that come from some types of sheep have more medulla than others. Wool fibers with medulla are coarser than those without.

▼ *This pile of fleece, or wool, has been freshly shorn from sheep.*

Wool Characteristics

Wool is known for the many important characteristics, or qualities, that make it desirable. Wool is made up of a protein called keratin. Keratin is also found in human nails and hair, and in animal hooves. Keratin makes a substance hard, or gives it strength. Wool is also water absorbent, which means it can soak up liquid. When wool is dyed, the dye is absorbed evenly to create richly colored yarn or thread. Wool's absorbency also makes it **resistant** to fire because the fibers hold moisture. Wool is also flexible and durable. It can be bent and stretched many times and still spring back into its original shape.

▼ *The cortex contains a pigment called melanin, which gives wool its color. The more melanin the fiber has, the darker colored the wool.*

A Cloth for all Seasons

Wool clothing is worn in both hot and cold climates. In cold climates, wool is made into sweaters, mitts, scarves, socks, and blankets. Wool keeps people warm by absorbing water that is in damp cold air and keeping it away from people's skin. Wool works much the same way to keep people cool in hot climates, too. When people sweat, wool absorbs the sweat and keeps it away from the skin. This helps keep the body at a constant temperature.

▶ *Until the 1940s, bathing suits were made from wool. These suits absorbed so much water that they became heavy and hard to swim in when wet.*

7

Wool Lands

Sheep are raised in countries around the world. Scientists believe that sheep originally came from the mountainous areas of Southwest Asia, from what is now Turkey to southern Iran. Sheep can survive in cold mountain areas and also in hot, arid deserts. Sheep will eat almost any kind of weed or grass, often the plants that other livestock will not eat. This makes them very **adaptable**.

Top Producers of Wool

Australia produces the most wool. Raising sheep for their wool is the country's most important form of land use. There are more than 114 million sheep in Australia, raised on over 70,000 large sheep farms called stations. Some stations have flocks of more than 100,000 sheep. Sheep are raised mainly in the drier areas of the country, where the climate is unsuitable for growing crops. China, the world's second largest wool-producing country, has the largest number of sheep, but produces less wool than Australia. Many of China's sheep are raised for their meat. In the third-largest wool producing country, New Zealand, sheep outnumber people two to one. Sheep farms in New Zealand are also called stations. Other large wool producing countries include Iran, the United Kingdom, and Argentina.

(below) This map shows where most of the world's wool is produced today. It also shows where sheep were originally raised.

United Kingdom · Russian Federation · Atlantic Ocean · Turkey · Iran · China · Pacific Ocean · Sudan · India · Indian Ocean · Equator · Argentina · Australia · New Zealand · Top 10 Producers of Wool · Early Areas of Wool Production

(above) Sheep are raised on sheep farms.

Top Consumers of Wool

China imports the most raw wool fiber, or wool as it comes off the sheep. To import something means to buy it from another country. China is one of the world's largest clothing and textile producers and exporters. This means that China brings in the raw wool, makes it into a finished product, and then sells, or exports it, to other countries in the world. Italy is the second largest importer of wool, followed by Germany and the United Kingdom. India, Korea, and Japan also import a lot of wool.

▶ *Many crafts are made of wool, such as knitted dolls.*

Raising Sheep

There are thousands of different types, or breeds, of sheep. Different sheep produce different types of wool, used for different purposes. Some sheep, such as Drysdale sheep, produce coarse wool, or wool that has thick fibers. Coarse wool is commonly used to make carpets. Other types of sheep, such as the Merino breed, produce finer wool, used to make clothing. Some sheep are raised for their meat, called mutton, and not for wool.

Sheep Pastures

Sheep eat many types of plants, such as grass, weeds, hay, and clover. They are grazing animals, which means that they eat plants close to the ground slowly over a period of time. Sheep graze for about seven hours a day. Their stomachs have four parts, so they belong to a family of animals called ruminants. Sheep eat plants and then regurgitate, or bring them up, chew them some more, and then swallow them again. The repeated chewing and **digesting** of their food is why sheep can eat plants that other animals cannot. On most farms, sheep are put out to graze in pastures. Farmers take care of their pastures, planting seed to make sure there is a correct balance of different kinds of food for the sheep to remain healthy. Often pastures are divided into different sections and the sheep are rotated from one section to another so that the plants have a chance to grow. During the winter in cooler climates, when the pastures are covered with snow, sheep are fed hay and some grain in barnyard troughs.

(above) Sheep are called ruminant species because they have four compartment stomachs. Cows are also ruminant species. Like cows, sheep chew their cud, or food, more than once.

▼ *Female sheep are called ewes. Male sheep used for breeding are called rams, and baby sheep are called lambs.*

Shepherds

On large sheep ranches or stations, sheep farmers often hire shepherds to keep track of their flocks. Shepherds ride on motorcycles or horseback and move the sheep from one pasture to another. In Australia, workers on sheep stations are called "Jackaroos" if they are men, and "Jillaroos" if they are women. These farm hands help care for the sheep and do other jobs, such as repairing broken fences on the sheep station.

Protecting and Guarding

Sheep naturally stay together in a flock. This makes it easy for shepherds to manage large numbers of sheep with few helpers. Dogs are some of the most important helpers in managing a flock of sheep. Certain breeds of dogs, such as Border Collies, are used to herd sheep. Border Collies get sheep to go where they want them to by staring at them, or giving them "the eye." This **intimidates** the sheep, so the dogs can direct them to where they want them to go. Other breeds of dogs, such as Great Pyrenees, are used to guard the flock. These large dogs are raised with lambs so that they learn to bond with and protect sheep. Some common sheep **predators** in North America are coyotes, dogs, cougars, and wolves. Donkeys and llamas can also be used to guard sheep. Other ways farmers protect their sheep is by using electric fences and pens.

(right) Shepherds commonly use Border Collie dogs to help them herd their flocks of sheep.

The Dingo Fence

Dingoes are wild dogs that live in Australia and prey on sheep. To protect the sheep flocks, a 3,300-mile (5,320-kilometer) long fence was built in the southeast of the country. The wire fence is six feet (1.8 meters) tall and is the longest fence in the world. While successfully keeping dingoes away from the sheep flocks, the fence also resulted in an explosion of rabbit and kangaroo populations in the southeast. Without the dingoes to keep their populations under control, the kangaroos and rabbits are eating up the pastures reserved for sheep.

Sheep Dipping

Sheep farmers work to ensure that their sheep have the best quality wool. They watch the sheep for signs of insects or pests, such as sheep keds and sheep lice, that can irritate the sheep causing them to scratch their fleece against fences or troughs and damage or tear the wool. Torn wool is worth less money. The farmers also watch to make sure the sheep are kept clean. Fleece that is soiled by urine or blood from cuts can become infected with maggots if flies lay their eggs there. This is called myiasis, or fly-strike. Once the maggots hatch, they begin to feed on the living **tissue** of the sheep. One way to keep sheep free from pests is sheep dipping. A sheep dip is a large, deep tub filled with water and insecticides, which are chemicals that kill insects. The sheep walk through the water and are "bathed" in the solution. Insecticides can also be applied in sprays and powders.

Spring Shearing

Lambs are first sheared when they are between three and 11 months old. This wool is called lamb's wool, and it is fine and soft. By the next shearing, between nine and 18 months, the wool fibers are thicker. After the third time sheep are sheared, their wool will stay the same thickness. Sheep live for about ten to 12 years and are shorn each year, usually in spring. Sheep can be sheared either by a professional shearer or by a robotic shearing machine. Recently, a drug has been developed that can be given to sheep to make them shed their wool.

▶ *Sheep keds are tick-like insects that use their piercing mouthparts to suck sheep's blood. The insects irritate the sheep's skin and make it itch.*

(below) Shepherds wear protective clothing while they guide their sheep through sheep dips. Sheep dips are used to kill any insects and other pests that live in the fleece of the sheep. The sheep are commonly immersed in the sheep dip more than once to make sure their fleece is fully cleaned.

Shearers and Wool Workers

People who shear sheep are called shearers. They are often part of a larger team of workers who go from farm to farm shearing sheep and sorting and baling the wool. Shearers are trained to remove the fleece from sheep without hurting the animal. They use mechanical blades to shave the sheep in a room in the barn kept clean for that purpose. Sheep shearers are often trained at universities and colleges. In some countries, sheep shearing competitions are held to see who can shear the most sheep in the fastest time. Experienced shearers can shear up to 20 sheep an hour. Once the wool had been sheared, it is pressed, weighed, and baled. The bales of wool are **branded** with the name of the farm and are ready to be sold.

(right) At sheep shearing competitions, contestants are judged on how fast they shear, the condition of the fleece, how the animal is handled, and how well the sheep looks.

Wool Sorter's Disease: Anthrax

Wool sorters shake the fleece to remove any loose dirt and other barnyard matter. They then sort the wool according to its color and fiber length and quality before it is pressed into bales. Sheep's fleece can carry a type of **bacteria** that sheep handlers breathe into their lungs. The bacteria causes a fatal disease called anthrax. Anthrax is also called Wool Sorter's Disease. Today, most sheep are **vaccinated** to prevent the spread of anthrax.

(left) A wool sorter shakes a Merino sheep fleece free from debris at a farm in Australia.

From Sheep to Sweater

Once wool has been baled and bagged it goes to a warehouse. Wool buyers sample the wool to test the length, thickness, and dirt content of the fleece. After testing, the wool is auctioned off, or sold to the highest bidder. Using computers and the Internet, some auctions are now held online.

Washing Wool

Wool is naturally covered in a greasy substance called lanolin. Sheep produce lanolin to make their fleece waterproof. Lanolin is removed before wool is processed by washing, or scouring, the fleece in soap and water. Washing the wool also removes any dirt. During washing, rakes move the wool first through warm soapy water, then through a cold-water rinse. Rollers squeeze the excess water from the fleece. It is then dried in a hot air drying chamber.

(top right)
Wool drying in the sun.

(right) Shorn wool is bundled and ready for auction.

(opposite page) Brightly-colored dyed wool is hung to dry in a market in Morocco.

Blending and Dyeing

Wool from different bales is blended together. This mixes wool that is slightly different colors and lengths to make a more uniform batch. Next, wool can be dyed. Wool that is dyed at this stage is called stock-dyed. During this stage, loose wool fibers are dyed in large vats. Dyeing fibers before they are made into cloth creates a more even-colored finished product.

Carding

Next, wool is carded. To card wool, the clean, dry fibers are passed through wire rollers. The rollers are different sizes and turn at different speeds. This action causes the fibers to be straightened and pulled into a thin web. The web is then pulled apart by long pieces of metal and rolled over one another to make a sliver. A sliver is a strand, or rope, of wool fibers.

Woolen and Worsted

After carding, wool can be processed in two different ways. Longer fibers are used to make worsted wool. Short, coarse fibers are made into cloth using the woolen process. In the woolen method of processing, the wool slivers are lightly twisted, or gathered, and wound into a ball. The lightly twisted fibers are called roving. The roving is ready for the next stage, which is spinning. Worsted wool is also spun, but there are more steps between carding and spinning. Wool that is worsted is combed and drawn, or stretched out, before spinning. These steps remove the shorter fibers and align the remaining longer fibers. Worsted wool ends up smoother and more compact.

Spinning

The wool fibers are then spun. Spinning twists the fibers into thread or yarn. Spools of roving are placed on the spinning machine and the ends are drawn through small rollers. The machine then twists and re-twists the roving into thread or yarn. Worsted yarn is tightly spun, and woolen yarn is spun looser.

▸ *Worsted wool is commonly used to make suits because it is smooth and crisp.*

(below) Wool is spun into thread and yarn by workers in factories.

16

Weaving and Knitting

Once yarn and thread have been made, they can be dyed and made into cloth. There are two main ways of making wool cloth, weaving and knitting. Weaving is done on a large frame called a loom. Weaving uses two threads, one going lengthwise across the loom, called the warp, and the other crosswise, called the weft. Passing the threads through each other causes a weave pattern to be formed. Knitting machines make cloth by interlocking rows of looped thread or yarn.

Fulling and Finishing

After wool has been made into fabric, it is shrunk in a process called fulling, or milling. During the fulling stage, moisture, heat, and friction are applied to the cloth. This causes the weave or knit to tighten. The finishing steps vary depending on the type of cloth and its intended use. For example, woolen cloth can be brushed to make the fibers' ends stand up. This makes soft and fluffy woolen cloth, such as flannel. Worsted cloth is often sheared or singed so that there are no loose ends. It has a smoother and crisper feel, and is used to make business suits and dresses. Chemical finishes are applied to the fabric. Some chemicals make wool machine washable, while others make it stain proof or fireproof.

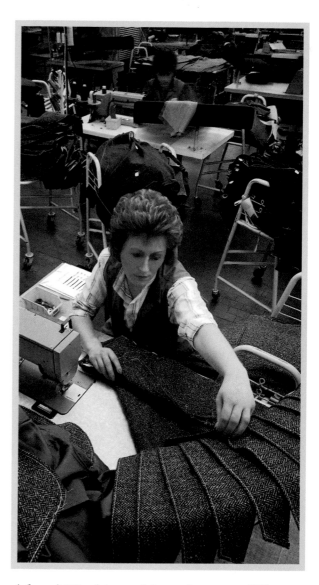

(above) Wool is used to make many different pieces of clothing. This worker is making wool coats in a factory.

Felt

Felt is another kind of wool cloth. To make felt, the wool fibers are pressed together using heat and moisture. This makes the fibers stick together. Wool can easily be made into felt because of the scaly cells on the fibers. Other animal furs are also used to make felt, such as beaver pelts.

Wool in Ancient Times

Sheep were domesticated, or raised as livestock, about 10,000 years ago. They were one of the first animals to be raised by people for their meat. The wool of early sheep was not like the wool of sheep today. These sheep had coarse outer hair and an undercoat that was used for wool. After many centuries of introducing sheep to new areas and breeding them with the wild sheep found there, the wool bearing sheep of today developed. Today's sheep are the result of breeding sheep from Southwest Asia with sheep from Europe.

▶ *Stone tablets found at ancient sites in Iraq were used to record the number of sheep and cows a farmer had.*

▼ *The common ancestor of the sheep breeds used for wool today is the mouflon from Central Asia. Mouflons have a wooly undercoat that they grow in winter. The rest of their bodies are covered in short hairs.*

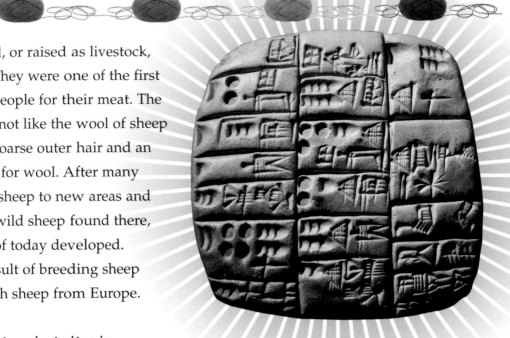

Mesopotamia's Wool

Mesopotamia is the name given to ancient Iraq. Historians believe Mesopotamia was the home of the world's first **civilization**. Sometime before 6,000 B.C., the people of Mesopotamia stopped traveling from place to place in search of food and settled on the land, farming and raising livestock. Among the livestock they raised were sheep. The earliest farmers in Mesopotamia wore the skins of sheep for clothing. Between 5000 and 4000 B.C., they started using the wool of sheep, which historians believe the Mesopotamians made into felt. Later, it was woven into cloth. Wool became an important export in Mesopotamia. It was traded west across the Syrian Desert to the Mediterranean, east to **Persia** and by boat across the Persian Gulf to India, and south across the Arabian Sea to Africa. Wool and barley were the main trade items of Mesopotamia.

Sheep Come to Greece

Sheep were introduced to ancient Greece from Central Asia. The ancient Greeks used sheep for wool, meat, and milk. In winter, the Greeks wore cloaks made of wool. The cloaks, called *peplos*, were large rectangular pieces of cloth that also served as blankets. Wool cloth and clothing could be bought in the agora, or marketplace, but it was expensive. Most people made their own wool clothing. Making clothing was the job of the female members of the household.

Wool Spreads with Empire

In **ancient Rome**, most clothing was made of wool. Women spun wool into threads and wove it into cloth in the home. Making wool cloth was also the job of household slaves. Wealthy Romans also bought expensive imported cloth, such as linen, cotton, and silk. Both tunics worn for everyday, and togas worn by important men were made from wool. The most important men in society wore robes with purple or crimson stripes. The purple dye for the stripes came from a type of shellfish and was very valuable. The wool fleece was dyed before it was spun into thread. The Romans bred only certain types of sheep to produce the finest types of wool. They then spread these breeds of sheep throughout Europe, including Spain and England, as they expanded their **empire**.

▲ *An ancient Roman wool garment worn by an important man, as shown by the purple stripe.*

(right) Archaeologists have uncovered many tools in England that were used to spin and weave wool, and to sew pieces of cloth together to make clothing. The tools are made from animal bones and deer antler.

Medieval Wool

During the period of history called the Middle Ages, which lasted from about 500 A.D. to 1500, raw wool and wool cloth became important commodities in Europe. Exporting raw wool to other European countries made both Spain and England wealthy. In some areas of Europe, thriving wool textile industries were built.

Spain's Mighty Merino

In the 700s, Spain was invaded by people from North Africa called Moors. The Moors established a trade in wool with North Africa, Greece, Egypt, and Turkey. They introduced a type of sheep that had been brought to North Africa and bred it with a sheep from Europe to make the Merino breed. Merinos have long, woolly coats all over their bodies and produce fine wool. Many sheep herds were owned by the Church or the **nobility**. Both of these groups were powerful and rich members of society, and grew richer from the sale of wool. Owners of large herds became known as Mestas. Spanish wool was exported all over Europe and used to make cloth. Until 1786, exporting Merino sheep out of Spain was punishable by death. This was because Spain wanted to keep its **monopoly** on Merino wool exports.

◀ *Medieval peasants shear sheep on a manor. A manor was a parcel of land, or estate, where peasants worked. Manors were owned by wealthy nobles.*

England's Staple

By the 1100s, raw wool was one of England's greatest exports. When a deadly plague called the "Black Death" swept through England in the mid-1300s, many peasants died. Peasants were poor farmers who grew crops for wealthier landowners, called nobles. With the shortage of peasant farmers, many English landowners transformed their farmland into pastures and began to raise more sheep. This caused wool exports to rise. The English king made money by taxing the export of wool. Wool was exported to Flanders, which is now part of France and Belgium, where it was made into cloth and sold at fairs all over Europe. The finished cloth was also sold back to England. English merchants soon realized that they could make more money by making the cloth themselves. In 1377, England's King Edward III stopped woven cloth from being imported into England and invited weavers from Flanders to come to England.

▼ *In the late 1200s, spinning wheels were in use in Europe. Historians believe the spinning wheel was first invented in India.*

Guilds

Guilds were groups of craftspeople that bonded together to ensure the quality of their craft. In Europe, there were many guilds related to the wool industry. There were guilds for wool merchants, as well as for wool craftspeople. In each wool-producing town, there were guilds for weavers, dyers, and fullers. The guilds ensured that only masters of the trade could sell the product. To become a master, craftspeople spent many years learning the trade as apprentices. Then, when they had met the requirements set out by the guild, the craftspeople could become masters and go into business for themselves.

(right) Guilds organized for wool workers decided how much members could charge for their goods.

Settlers and Sheep

The money Spain and England made from the export of wool helped finance voyages of exploration. Beginning in the 1400s, European countries began setting out to discover and settle new lands. They claimed land and set up **colonies** in the Americas, Africa, Asia, and Australia. Explorers and settlers introduced many new species of plants and animals, including sheep, to these lands.

(below) The Navajo native people from what is now the southern United States traded with the Spanish settlers and also raided their settlements and stole sheep. From the sheep's wool, the Navajo wove rugs and blankets.

Conquistadors' Sheep

Christopher Columbus was an explorer who reached the **New World**, in 1492. On his second voyage, in 1493, he introduced sheep to Cuba and the Dominican Republic. When the Spanish, led by conquistador, or conqueror, Hernando Cortez, took over the capital of Tenochititlan, present-day Mexico, and established the colony of New Spain in 1531, they brought sheep to the North American continent. The sheep were known as Churra sheep and had long shaggy coats. The sheep spread throughout North and South America as the Spanish expanded their settlements. They were first brought to the United States in 1598 by Spanish explorer Juan de Onate who set up a settlement in the Rio Grande Valley, now New Mexico.

North American Colonies

The English, Dutch, and French all set up settlements in North America in the early 1600s. The settlers brought sheep with them to use for their meat and to make cloth. England tried to prevent wool from being produced in its colonies so that it would not compete with England's wool exports. By the mid-1600s, sheep had become plentiful in the colonies. In 1699, the British government passed the Wool Act. This law prohibited exporting wool from the American colonies. American colonists proudly wore wool cloth that they had spun themselves, called homespun, in resistance to the English laws.

South Africa to Australia

The king of Spain gave Merino sheep to the Dutch in 1790 as a gift. These sheep were brought to the Cape Colony in what is now South Africa. From South Africa, two British officers brought sheep to Australia in 1797. Sheep had been introduced to Australia in 1788 with the "First Fleet," which is the name given to Australia's earliest ships carrying English settlers. The sheep brought with the First Fleet were covered in short hair, so they were used for their meat and not for wool. As settlements spread across Australia, the number of Merino sheep grew. Other breeds of sheep were introduced and bred with the Merino sheep. By 1879, there were about one million sheep in Australia. Today, Merino sheep are the most common type of sheep in Australia.

(above) This illustration shows an American wool carder combing wool. Wool carders used combs to disentangle the wool fibers before it could be spun into products, including clothing.

At Work in Wool Mills

Until the early 1800s, most wool was made into cloth in the home. In some areas, all the steps of wool processing took place at home, from sheep rearing to making clothing. People made just enough wool cloth to suit the needs of their families. In England, wool cloth making was a cottage industry. A cottage industry is one run by an **entrepreneur** who supplies the raw wool to each craftsperson in turn until the cloth is finished. Each craftsperson worked at their own home, and was paid by the entrepreneur according to the amount of product they produced.

Fulling Mills

Fulling was the first step in cloth processing to be done in **mills**. As early as the 1200s in Europe, wool cloth woven at home was taken to the fulling mill to be shrunk. Fulling tightened the weave and cleaned the cloth. The mills were situated beside waterfalls or streams that powered waterwheels. The waterwheels powered wooden, and later iron, mallets that beat the cloth in tubs. The cloth was then dried outdoors on tentering frames. The fulling mill was usually owned by the local monastery or by the noble who owned the land. The peasants who lived on the land paid to use the mill.

(above) The steps to process wool, including spinning and weaving wool, were a cottage industry, which means they were done in people's homes.

Big Ideas

Between 1790 and 1890, almost every step in wool processing became mechanized, or had new machines invented to do the job. The invention of the flying shuttle, which sped up weaving on looms, was the first to change the textile industry. The flying shuttle was invented by John Kay, in 1733, in England. It allowed more cloth to be woven in less time. In 1767, James Hargreaves invented the spinning jenny. The spinning jenny had more spindles holding more thread, allowing yarn to be spun more quickly. This resulted in more yarn and thread being spun than the weavers could keep up with.

Spinning and Carding

In 1778, English inventor Samuel Crompton combined the spinning jenny with another invention called the water frame, which used water power to spin thread faster, but used only one spindle at a time. Crompton's spinning mule allowed for more thread to be spun faster. The spinning mule was too large a machine to have in homes, so the spinning stage of processing began to be moved to mills. By 1775, carding was also mechanized. The first carding machine was invented in England in 1748. It was later improved upon by Richard Arkwright, who was also from England. Many of these inventions were first used in the cotton industry, but once applied to the wool industry, manufacturing quickly grew away from a cottage industry to mills, or factories.

(above) The use of machinery in wool mills decreased the time it took to weave wool products.

▼ *Samuel Crompton invented the spinning mule, which was used to spin wool threads. Crompton's original machine was very large, and was equipped with more than 140 spindles.*

The Final Weave

With carding and spinning taking place in mills, weaving was the only step in processing that was still mainly done in the home. In 1785, Edmund Cartwright from England invented the power loom. He also invented a combing machine. The combing machine aligned the wool fibers so they were parallel and removed the shorter fibers. The power loom was at first dependent on water power to operate. The first power looms were not very efficient. Over the next twenty years they were improved. By the beginning of the 1800s, the power loom was combined with a new power source, the steam engine. Using coal fires, the steam engine powered machinery in mills that did not have to be built near water. New factories were built across England.

The Luddites Fight Back

In 1811, a group of weavers near Nottingham, England, broke into a master weaver's shop that housed new mechanical looms. Using hammers and axes, they destroyed the machines. The weavers, who came to be called Luddites, were concerned that the new advances in technology would destroy their way of life. They were unhappy that machines were taking the jobs of people. With machinery, jobs that used to be done by five or six weavers could now be done by one. They were also unhappy that the new looms created lesser quality cloth. The Luddite movement spread to other English towns. By 1812, the English government had passed a law that made it illegal for anyone to destroy the machines. The government was also forced to send in soldiers to towns were Luddites were active to protect manufacturing.

◁ *A group of English weavers, called the Luddites, destroyed mechanical looms because they were afraid their work would no longer be needed.*

America's Woolen Mills

The first successful water-powered woolen mill was opened in Gray, Maine, in 1791. Samuel Mayall opened the mill after smuggling the plans out of England. England closely guarded its industrial advances to keep others from building mills and profiting from its machines. Other woolen mills opened in Massachusetts, Wisconsin, Missouri, Illinois, and other states.

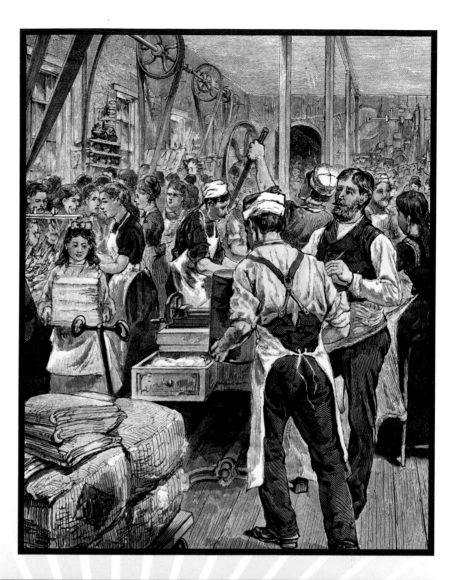

(right) Many wool mills were established in America during the 1800s, where many workers were employed.

Trade Blankets

Many British and American woolen mills made trade blankets. Trade blankets were used by European explorers and **trappers** to trade with Native North Americans. The blankets were also purchased with furs and native crafts at European trading posts. The Pendleton Woolen Mills company in Oregon was a wool mill that only made trade blankets. Native Americans prized the wool blankets because the wool was easier to wash and prepare than animal skins and furs. The blankets also became important to Native Americans as animals disappeared due to over hunting, and their skins, traditionally used to make clothing, grew scarce.

▲ *Trade blankets, such as this one, were important in the fur trade. Native peoples used them to make clothing such as coats.*

Uses of Wool

Wool is a versatile fabric, which means it can be used for a variety of purposes. Unlike many other fabrics, wool has not been replaced by synthetic materials. Synthetic materials are created by people in laboratories using chemical means. These materials are not found in nature. Often, synthetic materials are blended with wool to create specialty fabrics. Scientists have not yet developed a synthetic material that has all the qualities of wool.

Fabulous Felt

Felt has many different uses. Felt is used to cover collapsible circular tents first used by nomadic peoples in Central Asia and Mongolia. These tents are called *yurts* or *gers*. Felt is a good insulator, which means it is warm and traps heat. Felt is also a good absorber of sound and liquid. Felt is used on musical equipment such as pianos to keep wood and metal parts from clanking together. Felt pads are also used on automobiles and machinery.

Rugs and Other Home Furnishings

Wool has traditionally been used to make carpets. In Central Asia, in countries such as Turkey, Afghanistan, and Pakistan, wool carpet making is an art that dates back many centuries. The carpets are handwoven on looms. The wool comes from the Karakul sheep, which has long wool that is easily spun. Today, the carpets are still made by hand and in factories and exported around the world. Wool is also used to make mattress pads, which are often found in upholstery and seat covers.

▲ *This carpet was made in Persia, present-day Iran, in the 1500s. It is made of wool, cotton, and silk.*

(below) Felt is added to the hammers inside pianos, which are the parts that strike against the steel strings to produce sound.

Wool and You

Wool is used in many everyday products. How many of these wool products do you have around you right now?

◀ **Tennis balls and baseballs**

▶ **Knitted sweaters, mitts, scarves, and hats**

▼ **Markers and felt tip pens**

▼ **Knitted craft items and puppets made with yarn**

The Future of Wool

Some types of livestock farming have been taken over by large corporations in recent years, such as cattle and pig farming. Sheep farming is still run by independent farmers, whose flocks number anywhere from a few hundred to thousands of sheep. This means that farmers make the important decisions about how to care for their sheep.

(below) Sheep farmers do their best to care for their flocks. Sheep raised on arid lands need more grazing land than sheep in other climates because there are less plants for them to eat. Farmers make sure that there are enough plants on their farms for their sheep to eat.

Sheep and the Environment

Sheep farmers care about the environment. Without clean air, soil, and water, their sheep will not be healthy. There are concerns about the effects of chemicals used in sheep dipping running off into the earth and poisoning the soil and groundwater. Sheep also produce a lot of methane gas as they digest their food. The methane is released into the atmosphere, or air, when sheep belch or pass gas. Methane is a gas that contributes to **global warming**. Countries around the world are trying to lower their greenhouse gas emissions. In places like Australia, where a lot of sheep are raised, methane gas adds to the amount of greenhouse gases they produce.

Sheep Breeding

Sheep have become what they are today by a process called selective breeding. In selective breeding, only certain sheep with desirable qualities are allowed to breed. This is why sheep with long, soft woolly coats are now raised. Scientists are continuing to experiment with sheep breeds. In Australia, scientists are trying to develop a breed of sheep that will shed their wool without having to be sheared. They are also developing sheep breeds that are resistant to worms and diseases.

Animal Welfare

Mulesing is a sheep farming practice that animal welfare activists are trying to have stopped. Mulesing is done by some Australian sheep farmers to prevent sheep from being infested with maggots. The farmers surgically remove the folds of skin from around the sheep's tails so that flies cannot lay their eggs there. This practice is painful for the sheep. Sheep farmers in Australia are looking for alternative ways to prevent the infestations.

(above) These socks are made from organic wool. For wool to be considered organic, the sheep must not undergo sheep dipping, and their feed must not be treated with chemicals, such as pesticides.

▼ *Mulesing is done to prevent maggot infestations.*

(right) An activist for the People for the Ethical Treatment of Animals (PETA) protesting against the practice of mulesing.

Glossary

adaptable Able to adjust to fit new conditions

ancient Rome A civilization that lasted from 753 B.C. until 476 A.D.

bacteria Tiny, single-celled organisms

brand To mark a product with the name or symbol of the manufacturer

cells Small units that make up all living things

civilization The way of life of a group of people in history

colony Land ruled by a distant country

digestion The process in which the body breaks down food into nutrients

elasticity Ability to return to a normal shape after being stretched

empire A group of countries under one ruler

entrepreneur A person who organizes and operates a business

export To sell goods to another country

fiber A long, thin strand of natural material

global warming An increase in the Earth's temperatures caused by pollution

insulator Material that prevents the flow of heat into or out of an object

intimidate To make timid or fearful

Middle Ages The period from about 500 A.D. to 1500 in western Europe

mill A building or factory equipped with machines for producing a product

monopoly Control over a commodity

New World The name given to North, Central, and South America by Europeans

nobility Members of the most powerful or wealthy group in a society

parliament An elected governmental body that makes laws for a country

Persia The present-day country of Iran, to the west of Afghanistan

predator An animal that eats other animals

process To change from its original form and made into something else

protein Chemicals necessary for growth and health

resistant Able to defend against fire or disease

shear To remove wool from animals with tools

tissue A group of cells that perform a similar function

trapper A person who traps animals for their fur

vaccinate To give a preparation to bring on immunity against a disease

Index